marriage: five years later

lessons from the early years

Alan Seaborn

Copyright © 2019 Alan Seaborn. All rights reserved.

Published by Winning At Home, Zeeland, Michigan;

www.winningathome.com

ISBN: 978-1-7326465-1-3

Unless otherwise indicated, Scripture quotations are taken from the Holy Bible, New International Version®, NIV® Copyright ©1973, 1978, 1984, 2011 by Biblica, Inc.® Used by permission. All rights reserved worldwide.

Scripture quotations marked MSG are taken from The Message Copyright © 1993, 1994, 1995, 1996, 2000, 2001, 2002 by Eugene H. Peterson.

Cover design by Winning At Home

Interior design by Winning At Home

For Annaliese

Thanks for your partnership on this journey. I'm looking forward to our next five years together!

Thank you to the couples and individuals who have invested in our marriage, whether directly or indirectly. A friend once told me that good marriages are contagious, so thanks for living out the examples that rubbed off on Annaliese and me!

Table of Contents

Preface		9
Introduction		11
1	Be Completely Humble	17
2	And Gentle	31
3	Gentleness in Practice	57
4	Be Patient	69
5	Bearing with One Another in Love	79
6	Living It Out	93

Preface

Since the title and subtitle of this book make it obvious, I don't think I need to say that I'm not an expert on marriage. You already know I'm not. Nor am I writing about marriage because Annaliese and I have a picture-perfect marriage. We don't. We've run into many of the same challenges a lot of newly married couples run into—and we're still dealing with them. Mixing two lives together is tricky!

I do, however, want to start off with a funny story about my obvious lack of expertise.

Winning At Home, the ministry I'm part of that's based in West Michigan, hosts a Legacy Luncheon every fall for couples in the area who have been married for fifty or more years. We want to not only celebrate them but thank them for the example they set for coming generations. They've shown us that marriage can last.

I've emceed the event for the past few years, and the first year I felt weird about speaking to couples who had been

Marriage: Five Years Later

married for far longer than I'd been alive! I decided to open with a joke about how if you've been married for only two and a half years like me, half a year is a big deal—kind of like when kids tell you they're five and three quarters years old. But as soon as I said, "I've been married for two and a half years," the audience started laughing. I was kind of thrown! That was just the set up for my punch line, but they found the two and a half years laughable on their own.

I didn't take their response personally, but I did consider it instructive. The lesson was clear: I didn't have much credibility to speak about marriage because of my limited experience. Yet after a year or so, I decided the lessons Annaliese and I were learning early in our marriage were still valuable. And in many ways, this book is the result. While bedrock truths will probably play out in different ways as we get further down the road as a couple, and while for sure our understanding of them will deepen, those truths will never change.

So that's our starting point for this book. I'll share about what Annaliese and I have learned during the first five years of our marriage, and we pray that God will use our failures, successes, and growth to challenge and encourage you in your own marriage.

Introduction

I've talked to many couples who've had this same experience. When people found out Annaliese and I were engaged, many of them got a serious look on their faces and said, "Marriage is a lot of work." After hearing that over and over, I thought, *Man, they aren't doing a good job of celebrating with us and selling us on the idea of marriage!*

I know these people meant well when they told us that marriage would be a lot of work, but they seemed to be almost trying to talk us out of getting married. It felt both demoralizing and confusing to me. And maybe they just wanted us to have realistic expectations, but instead they made me wonder if their own marriages were bad. If that's the first thing someone says to you when they hear you're engaged, it's hard to take it any other way. I agree that our marriage has taken work, but that's not the first thing that pops into my head when I think about marriage!

In the chapters to come, I *will* discuss the work marriage has required of us but not from a pessimistic perspective. Instead, I'll share about how the work we've put in to understand each other, share life together, and sacrifice our own wants and needs for each other's wants and needs has brought about a whole new level of depth, intimacy, and caring. This is a subtle difference, but I'm wired to focus more on the *benefit of the effort* than on *the effort itself*.

Annaliese and I approach marriage from a faith-based perspective, and we've found great guidance and wisdom for our relationship in Scripture. It's also important for you to know that my fundamental understanding of what marriage is all about is shaped less by passages directly about marriage than by my understanding of what God is like and what he wants from us. Let me give an example.

Genesis 2:24, the verse about a man leaving his father and mother to be united to his wife, is *about* marriage. But 1 Corinthians 13, which is not about marriage but about love, teaches us what marriage is *all about*. Do you see the distinction? Much of Scripture tells us how people should interact with one another. And that's what marriage is—two people interacting as they build a life together that, of course, includes other people as well—families of origin, possibly children, friends, and other relationships with neighbors, coworkers, bosses, or employees.

Introduction

The Bible is filled with passage after passage of wisdom and insight when it comes to relating to other people. Even though many of them aren't specifically about marriage, when we remember that marriage is a relationship like any other, just on another level of intimacy, we realize that those verses still apply to how we live life with our spouse. The fruit of the Spirit (Galatians 5:22–23) should be evident in our marriage relationship. So should Jesus's command to "Love your neighbor as yourself" (Matthew 22:39) and Paul's teaching to "Forgive as the Lord forgave you" (Colossians 3:13). If we're not giving our marriage much thought, we might be putting it in a category so separate from any other relationship that we forget that the foundation of marriage is relationship.

With that in mind, Ephesians 4:2, the verse we'll unpack in this book, is one of my favorite verses that can be applied to marriage: "Be completely humble and gentle; be patient, bearing with one another in love." Now, it's much easier to plan on living out this verse than it is to actually practice it, but we all know every single relationship in our lives would be better if we approached every interaction with people with this verse as our blueprint. And if that's true of every relationship, it will for sure be true when it comes to marriage. After all, our husband or wife will know us on a deeper level than anybody else has. They'll see us at our best and at our worst. They'll see us at our most hopeful and joyful, but they'll also see us at our most vulnerable and disappointed. Sharing our lives with someone opens us up to both the thrill of victory and the agony of defeat. And because of the closeness of this relationship, our spouse will notice things about us no one else has—or at least no one has ever pointed out to us.

Some of what our spouses tell us will be great. They'll compliment us on some action or characteristic or on the color of our eyes or the shape of our knee or something even weirder. But they'll also notice some negative things about us. They'll comment on our habit of running behind schedule, or of pushing through other people's feedback to do what we wanted to do anyway, or of some strange idiosyncrasy no one else has ever mentioned.

Our response to the positive is to bask in the praise and the recognition. We always knew we were more special than anybody gave us credit for! The problem is that the critiques or criticisms have the opposite effect. We feel defensive, and our first thought is probably something along the lines of *Well, nobody else has ever complained about that! Sounds like a* you *problem to me!* That's because our first, and most natural, response is to deny that we have a problem and to try to redirect our shame and guilt at failure to other people—in this case, to our spouses.

As I share about our marriage and look at each part of Ephesians 4:2, my guess is you'll see some aspects of your own marriage. Maybe those glimpses won't be too flattering, but that's okay! The starting point has to be identifying potential growth areas. That's an embarrassing and exposing process, but it's the only way to begin the process of growth!

One final thought: change comes only when we change our *patterns of behavior*. At a premarital event Winning At Home hosted recently, WAH counselor Steven Kreitzer shared this about communication: "It's important to remember that *concepts* don't change anything. *Applying* these concepts to our lives is what brings the change." I couldn't agree more. Let's not just look for concepts as we move forward; let's take steps to make our marriages better!

CHAPTER ONE

Be Completely Humble

Be completely humble and gentle; be patient, bearing with one another in love.
Ephesians 4:2

Paul opens Ephesians 4:2 with a call to "be completely humble," a high calling.

Completely. Some of you probably started experiencing tightness in your chest even as you read these words. I'm experiencing that tightness as I'm writing them, because, I admit, I prefer a slightly (or more than that!) inflated view of myself and how flawlessly I think I'm moving through the world. From a realistic perspective, that's not true. But it sure feels good to tell myself that story.

Stories Affect Us

Stories we tell ourselves over and over present a big problem—we start to believe them. And then they make their way in so deep that they eventually become reality to us. Here's an example that will make this point. It's ridiculous, but hopefully it will show how we can believe what's not true if we buy into a false story.

When I was little, someone in my family (I don't remember who for sure) taught me a "fact" about moths. I was told if you touch a moth's wings and get dust from them on your fingers, that dust can make its way to your eyes if you rub them, which would make you go blind. I don't know if I was told that because I was trying to catch moths and they didn't want me to or if they were told this same ridiculous myth when they were a kid and believed it, but I doubt anyone reading this has ever heard of this idea.

I was either in high school or college when I learned the truth—that this was a made-up story, that moths aren't the blindness-causing, horror-inspiring insects I had always thought they were. They're basically just ugly butterflies. But the damage was done. My fear of moths had sunk too deep, and it persists to this day. I wouldn't quite call it a phobia, but I'm physically uncomfortable when I see a moth, and I can't make myself mentally relax until I know it's been removed from my immediate area. I don't know if I would touch a moth and then touch my eyes for any amount of money even though I rationally and objectively know it wouldn't pose any danger to me.

My moth experience doesn't connect directly to humility, but I think it illustrates the potential impact of stories we tell ourselves over and over. It's not all that difficult for a wrong perception to build over time until it turns into our reality, even when our version of reality isn't based on facts. That's when being completely humble comes into play. As I mentioned in the Introduction, our spouses will see (and point out) our blind spots, and that will feel awful. Nobody likes having holes poked in their version of reality. But blind spots revealed and holes poked aren't acts of hostility toward us. They're an opportunity to ensure that our perception of reality lines up a little bit more with actual reality. And having our shortcomings, failures, flaws, and blind spots pointed out is the painful process that we have to go through to make that happen.

How the World Sees Humility

In the culture Paul was writing to, humility wasn't considered a virtue. But it's not really considered a virtue in our culture either, if we're honest. We pretend we want people to be humble in victory and gracious in defeat, but then we celebrate bombastic self-promotion and reward the most self-aggrandizing people in our world. We like our sports superstars to hit the right mix of "confident" and "not too full of themselves," but we can excuse a failure of the latter after a big win. I'll admit that I enjoy seeing athletes yelling "You can't guard me!" to their hapless defender.

But we don't fall into valuing the opposite of humility only when it comes to sports. Reality TV is all about who can be the most over the top in their attention seeking. Some game shows and competitions even have pre-show auditions before they "randomly" choose a contestant in the moment. Right after high school, I went out to California with some friends, and we went to a taping of *The Price Is Right*. They had five to ten people go in front of the producers at a time because they wanted to know who would be excitable enough if they got on the show. A panel of four boring people guessing a price wouldn't make for good TV!

On the news, on our game shows and reality TV shows, at our sports events, and in so many other public venues, then, we see people who might not be acting proud, which we think of as the opposite of humility, but who definitely aren't coming across as humble. Seeing that over and over normalizes something that doesn't work very well when it comes to interpersonal relationships.

What Is True Humility?

Nobody ever taught me this explicitly; I just picked up bits and pieces that eventually shaped my idea. But I used to have a completely wrong understanding of humility. For about the first thirty years of my life, I thought a key aspect of humility was not accepting compliments because that would be prideful. If somebody told me I did a good job with something (even if I agreed!), I redirected the compliment. I passed the credit along to somebody else, or minimized the amount of work I'd done, or downplayed the finished product.

I eventually came to a new understanding by a surprising path. One of my hobbies is painting. I'm not a professional, but I've been doing it for a while now, and I'm usually pleased with how my work turns out. That presented a weird situation for me. If someone complimented me on one of my paintings, I had to either accept the compliment or pretend that I didn't like the painting as much as I did. But because I thought accepting a compliment was the equivalent of pride, I usually said something along the lines of "Oh, it's not that great" or "I just couldn't figure out this one part; look at how bad the ears look!" or "I'm getting better, but I have a long way to go."

Then one day I realized that if I ever showed one of my paintings to someone who shared my hobby, unless they were a better painter than I was, I was basically telling them their work was trash. That made me reexamine what humility really means, because being humble couldn't possibly mean I was supposed to lie to people! As I looked into it, I found a definition that made sense to me—the idea that humility is a modest, accurate view of yourself and your accomplishments. It's not humble to say you're bad at something you're good at. Humility means having an accurate understanding of *how* good at something you are. My paintings might not compare to those of professional artists and lots of other hobbyists, but that doesn't make them bad.

I think others have the same misguided ideas about humility I had. Instead of believing we should never take a compliment, humility is having an accurate understanding of our strengths and faults, to know what we're good at, what we're average at, and what we're bad at. In that sense, part of humility is about acknowledging reality.

That doesn't seem so hard when we're talking about painting or something else that's not too important. But when we run into opportunities to practice this acknowledgment of reality in our marriages, we have a whole different situation!

Practicing Humility in Marriage

Not too long after gaining this new understanding of what humility means, I had the chance to practice it in my marriage. Winning At Home periodically offers cruises for fifty to sixty married couples, and we had a cruise coming up in a few weeks where I was scheduled to speak. I went online to complete the registration details that would make boarding the ship much smoother, and I pulled out Annaliese's and my birth certificates, passports, driver's licenses, and the info on flights and hotels the cruise line wanted.

When I got to the point of entering passport information, I had no issue with Annaliese's. But although I thought I had a clear memory of renewing my passport a couple of years earlier (you probably already figured out where this is going), my passport was expired!

It was a Sunday evening, so I couldn't even get in touch with someone to figure out what I should do. I was sitting on the living room couch going through all the thoughts and emotions you might imagine: *How fast is the turnaround time for an expedited passport? Where is the nearest passport office that offers overnight passports? How much will this cost me? I can't miss this cruise; it's not just a vacation—I'm speaking!*

Those and a bunch of similar thoughts ran through my mind in the first few moments, but then I remembered I had the cell phone number of the head of the travel agency who was lining up everything for the cruise. Maybe he could help! I sent him a text explaining the situation and asking for his advice. My anxiety worsened at this point, because although my phone said the text had been read, I got no response. Was my situation such a lost cause that it wasn't even worth an answer? He's also a pastor, though, so I tried to convince myself that he was just in the middle of a Sunday night service. But that didn't do much to calm me down.

Then Annaliese walked into the room. I'm generally good at taking challenges in stride and rolling with the punches, but I was upset and worried about this one. That must have been written all over my face, because my wife immediately stopped and asked what was wrong.

"I thought I already renewed it," I said, "but apparently my passport is expired."

"Oh man, those are hard to get!"

She didn't mean it in a negative way; she was just sharing her first reaction. But that's still an example of a code-red moment, isn't it? We all know how it feels to be confronted with our own shortcomings. So here I was, with a great chance to practice humility, but I chose the sarcastic route instead: "Yeah, thanks a lot."

Humility doesn't come easy, does it?

Be Completely Humble

Whether or not we like it, we'll get the chance to practice humility in our marriages again and again. In this situation, I was already feeling pressured, ashamed, and exposed because of my mistake. And then I reacted in frustration because my mistake became obvious to Annaliese, and that threatened my image of myself. That might seem like over psychologizing or using a fancy word for an ugly thing, but I do think it's a good description of what happened.

If we don't practice being "completely humble" as Paul encourages us to—even when we make mistakes and especially in our marriages—our reaction is to minimize our mistakes and try to downplay the impact they make on us and our spouse. When we're hiding, we spend so much energy on staying hidden. It's also easy to keep hiding with an apology like "Sorry that I lashed out, but what you said made me feel [fill in the blank]" that allows us to "apologize" while still holding the higher ground. After all, we did what we did *because* of what they did, right? But that's not an apology; it's an excuse, a justification. A non-apologizing apology often does more damage and creates more hurt than not apologizing in the first place. This is the tricky part of a relationship—to genuinely apologize while also addressing what was hard for us.

I doubt you need any more convincing that not being completely humble can do damage to a marriage relationship. I also don't think you need more examples of a lack of humility. Instead, you probably want practical ways to not just manage conflict with humility but to avoid it in the first place!

A Tool for Deactivating Conflict: The Conflict Postmortem

If it's off limits to discuss the context around the conflict, that doesn't help. Both the offender and the offended are likely to need to talk about why they did what they did, said what they said, or felt what they felt. But if this discussion isn't managed carefully, it can turn into a whole new conflict about guilt, manipulation, or justification.

Annaliese and I have found a tool for deactivating conflict in the moment. I call it the Conflict Postmortem. The conversation begins with a genuine apology from one or both of us and leads to us talking about how the conflict started. The point of this part of the conversation isn't to find excuses or justifications but to look back on the conflict and its escalation to figure out what exactly went on. We look at how the situation and our reactions played into what happened, what happened, why it happened, how we felt as it was happening, and how we can avoid a similar situation in the future.

Thinking of the apology and the postmortem as two distinct parts of the conversation has been a helpful way for us to recognize what's happening. If the concept of this tool is new for you and your spouse, you might benefit from verbalizing the transition from apology to postmortem. If it's not clear to both of you what's going on, the postmortem part of the conversation can feel like excuse making.

This has been a hugely helpful tool for us, but we don't always practice it! You'd think that seeing how much this method helps us communicate clearly with each other would ensure that we'd use it. But it hasn't. It's interesting to me how often I find myself doing something that seems completely irrational *even to me!* If I have access to a helpful way of discussing conflict, why would I try to do it a way that's been proven *not* to work time after time?

The next time you find yourself in conflict with your spouse, give the Conflict Postmortem a try. We'll try to do the same!

Two Ways to Actively Practice Humility

Here are two practical ways to actively practice humility to avoid or avoid escalating some of those moments of conflict.

Marriage: Five Years Later

1. Don't be so quick to make your point.

Earlier I asked why I would try to deal with conflict in a way that's been proven not to work. The reason is the same reason all of us would give—when I'm caught up in the moment, I think I need to make my point. I think I have to refute Annaliese's ideas that I don't agree with, and I think I have to be right!

It's easy and natural to think that our own ideas and opinions are so important and valuable that we need to get them out of our heads and into the heads of the people around us. That's one of the biggest obstacles I run into when it comes to being humble. But when I practice not being so quick to make my point, I find it makes a big difference in my relationship with Annaliese. When I don't get so hung up on my own ideas, I do a much better job of listening to what she's saying. As I'm writing this, it was just yesterday that we ran into an issue as a result of me wanting to make sure Annaliese heard my perspective even though expressing it came at the expense of unity. If I had been more willing to hear what she was saying and why she was saying it, I could have avoided the conflict I caused by being in such a hurry to make my point.

2. Learn to think in terms of *we* instead of *me*.

Before I met and started seriously dating Annaliese, I did pretty much whatever came naturally to me: I made all the decisions about what to eat, how to spend my money, what to do with my free time, how to deal with disappointment, and so on. The key thread through all those decisions was that for twenty-seven years, even if I wasn't thinking in only selfish terms, *I* was the decision maker, and I was thinking in terms of *me*.

Learning to think in terms of *we* after doing that for so long has been an adjustment! It has played out in big ways that I'll talk about in this book, but it has also played out in small and less significant ways. I'll mention a couple of the more insignificant ways to illustrate how often we need to practice moving from *me* thinking to *we* thinking. Annaliese doesn't like the car to have less than a quarter tank of gas, while I'm comfortable driving with the gas light on for a bit. She doesn't mind half-read books or in-process projects lying around the house, while I like items to be put away when they're not being used. These examples aren't a big deal, and we haven't allowed them to become a big deal, but I mention them to illustrate how often we need to practice moving from *me* thinking to *we* thinking.

These two hands-on ways to practice humility are just the tip of the iceberg. If we keep a lookout and stay intentional about being completely humble in our relationship with our spouse, we'll see opportunity after opportunity present itself. These opportunities will often come up when we feel completely justified in being self-focused, and that's when we need to be the most intentional about taking Paul's words to heart.

CHAPTER TWO

And Gentle

*Be completely humble and gentle; be patient,
bearing with one another in love.*
Ephesians 4:2

The first thing that comes to mind when I think of gentleness is cautiously caring for something or someone. We're gentle with babies and children, and we're also gentle with small and fragile animals. Generally, cuteness brings out our desire to be gentle, doesn't it? But we aren't gentle just with living things; I'm gentle with my phone when I take it out of its case to clean it!

It's easy to see the connection between a baby, a small animal, and a case-less phone—they're all fragile and need our care to be protected and healthy. We treat them with gentleness because we value them. We make sure we prevent any harm from coming to them. And I think this helps us get to the core of what gentleness looks like in a marriage. Our partner and our relationship with them are valuable, so we treat them with gentleness to prevent any harm coming to them.

Our Home Renovation Challenge

The need to be gentle with Annaliese really hit home for me about four years into our marriage, during a home renovation. We had everything timed perfectly. We closed on our new house, the one we were renovating, a month ahead of when we had to be out of the house we were selling. And we were told by the guy doing the renovation that we could move into the new house the day we had to be out of our old one. It was the perfect *plan*—except his estimate was really bad! About a week before we were supposed to move, we were told to find a place to stay for "a few weeks."

We moved in with Annaliese's parents, and soon it became obvious that the new timeline was off too. After "a few weeks" at her parents' place, we moved in with my parents for a few more weeks. We moved back and forth between them on roughly that schedule for more than four months, living out of suitcases in our parents' basements with a puppy less than a year old in tow! At the same time, I was also doing a lot of work on our renovation myself, but I'll get to that.

I don't know how many of you have lived with a parent or parents when you were in your thirties, but if you have, you know what a challenge that can be. It's not that we don't get along with our parents, and it's not that their homes weren't nice (both sets of parents had a nicer place for us to stay than the home we sold or the home we were moving into!). It's just that living in somebody's basement is strangely hard. I'm an introvert; I need space to myself to relax and recharge. As you can imagine, living in somebody else's house makes finding that difficult. The rhythms of life I'd grown used to no longer existed. Erratic work and social schedules at both homes made pinning down and establishing new rhythms nearly impossible.

This meant that in addition to working on the new house as much as I could, I was also losing out on the time and space that would allow me to catch my breath and get back to having full energy. It's an overused phrase, but I felt like I was burning the candle at both ends. I would work my normal job, do everything I possibly could at the house, and then go "home" to a place where I didn't feel settled, to take a shower, grab a late dinner, and sleep.

At the same time, Annaliese had recently started an online course in life coaching. In addition to the stress of a regular work schedule, renovation responsibilities, and being displaced, she had classes, group meetings, clients to coach, and homework. And remember, we still had a puppy who was under one year old!

But there's more to this story than living in someone else's home. I'm wired to put my head down and just power through whatever I'm faced with. My natural response was to head over to the house almost every night after work and chip away at the renovation work I could do myself—as much as was possible for somebody with no actual construction skills. Even now, I'm still surprised at how many things I was able to come up with. I became a part-time demolition guy, cleaner, painter, part order-er, general contractor, and whatever else I could be. That wasn't always a good thing, though, because Annaliese isn't wired the same way. She needed times when we weren't focused completely on the house, moments when we just spent time together.

But I ended up leaning pretty heavily toward my own natural tendency of working at the house and powering through while Annaliese found comfort in the moments when we'd grab a cup of coffee on the way to Lowe's or have lunch in the backyard on a work break and call that a mini-date. If those moments were the "quality time" that we spent together, you can see that I didn't do a good job of valuing her needs while I was focusing on the immediate task of getting this work done.

Different Needs and Approaches
In the middle of all that craziness, we had plenty of opportunity to practice being gentle by meeting each other's needs! Even while I felt the need to work on the house,

we had to figure out how to get quality time together, how to have meaningful conversations (that weren't *only* about the house or the puppy, which sounds dumb, but it was weirdly hard!), how to prioritize each other, and how to stay sane. I'd give us a C, overall. But the crazy thing about marriage is that, sometimes, that's just the way it is, so you have to figure out how to adjust to it and make life work. When I talk to engaged and other newly married couples who are trying to figure out how to navigate difficult situations, I often remind them that this is what they signed up for.

But as I already mentioned, our needs and approaches to this situation weren't the same. It may be more natural for men to zone in on work like I did, sometimes to the detriment of our relationships. But the thing that makes it so challenging is that, in our minds, we're doing all the work *for* the good of our relationships. And I don't even think that's a rationalization. I think it's the difference between being goal-oriented and being people-oriented. Obviously, this isn't true of all men or all relationships, but men are often driven by a need to accomplish, to take the wildness of our surroundings and tame it. That's why our natural tendency is toward *fixing* rather than *listening*. Toward *doing* rather than *being*. And toward *journeying* rather than *enjoying the journey*.

Neither of those juxtapositions are healthy when we live at either extreme for prolonged periods of time. When it came to our budget, my approach was to live a spartan-like experience and cut the budget to the bone to pay off school loans and save. And when it came to our renovation, my approach was to spend all my free time working on the house, all while saying, "Yeah, it's extreme, and we're not spending a ton of time together enjoying life, but I'm doing this *for us!*"

The problem is when only one of the people involved in that "us" sees it that way, and I'm guessing that most people reading this can relate to the disconnect that can happen in the middle of a situation where one of you thinks it should be powered through and the other would like to enjoy life in the meantime. What I've seen is that typically women are more attuned to the opposite side of that spectrum I mentioned before. They're more oriented toward *listening* than *fixing*. Toward *being* more than *doing*. And toward *enjoying the journey* more than *journeying*. Again, living in either of these extremes isn't good or healthy.

The good news, though, is that if one partner is more geared toward one end of the spectrum and the other more toward the other end, they have a good chance of helping to balance each other out. They'll figure out how to achieve but not at the cost of neglecting people or relationships. They'll figure out how to enjoy and appreciate being with people, but not at the cost of *only* doing that and not making and executing plans.

Of course, there will be seasons of life when circumstances tilt (or force!) things in a certain direction. But if those seasons drag on too long, that creates strain and stress on a relationship. We certainly don't want to burn out our partner by living exclusively on our side of the spectrum for too long!

Spending Time Together

As I mentioned before, it's easy for me to zero in on the task at hand and give that most or all of my energy, leaving Annaliese with the leftovers. I just kept pushing and pushing on the house because it needed to be done. Annaliese was having a hard time with this, but I told her I couldn't relax and enjoy life when there were things at the house I should be working on.

We went on like that for a while—me working too much and her wishing we could connect more meaningfully. You see the complexity here, right? We both had valid reasons for thinking and feeling the way we did. That didn't make the challenge to practice gentleness by meeting each other's needs any easier, though, and we had to make a change. I'm also guessing our experience is relatable to some part of your relationship. One of you probably is more connection focused, the other is probably more project focused, and the difference in your priorities has probably caused some confusion, frustration, and disconnect at some point like it did for us.

The key to getting through these difficult times is remembering the importance of spending time *together*. Gentleness, often expressed through time spent together, breathes life into a relationship!

Dates

I finally agreed to go on a date (as long as I had a guarantee that we would keep it short!), and as we were driving to one of our favorite places to grab a quick bite to eat, I could see how excited and relieved Annaliese was. We agreed that we wouldn't talk about the house, allowing ourselves to get out of those worries for a couple of hours, and we did pretty well at avoiding that topic! We found (or maybe I found what Annaliese already knew) that we needed that time to connect and just enjoy hanging out with each other. Instead of talking about when the drywall guy was going to come and how much it would cost, we talked about Annaliese's life coaching program and how excited she was about starting to see clients. Instead of talking about the budget and what color we wanted our couch to be, we talked about how we were looking forward to using our space to entertain and get to know our new neighbors over dinner in our new home.

In short, it was hugely beneficial *for us*. I wasn't making progress on my goal of getting more of the house project done, but we were growing closer as a couple, which was more important even if I didn't see that at first.

Vacations

I've become convinced that vacations are hugely important—even for those of you who are way more driven than I am. But even the idea of vacationing was kind of foreign to me when Annaliese first brought it up. I had grown up taking vacations with my family, but I hadn't taken any since college—for close to ten years. I generally used vacation time at the end of the year before it expired so that I could spend a week or two staying up late, sleeping in, and lounging around the house. I always ended up feeling aimless and antsy to get back to work, though, so I never looked forward to "vacation" as an adult.

When Annaliese and I went on our first real vacation, I did it because I could tell she needed to just check out from the regular flow of life. I thought I was going just for her. But when we drove down to Florida and stayed near the beach for a week, where we just got to enjoy spending time together with no responsibilities to keep us occupied, it was so good. We had conversations that didn't normally come up, talking through some important and not-so-important things and just getting on the same page. That week was great for both of us. I even sort of learned what it looked like for me to relax and enjoy a vacation instead of just feeling like every day was a day I could have been home.

I'm mindful of the fact that not everyone has paid vacation days, and I'm aware that budgets and real concerns about money can be limiting factors for many people. That's been the case for us as well. During our home renovation, we couldn't afford to take an actual vacation, so we did a staycation and just enjoyed being together at home.

We slept in and relaxed, but we were also intentional about not passing each day just watching Netflix. Since we were still in the middle of the renovation, we'd spend three hours in the morning working on the house and then go out for an afternoon coffee date followed by dinner and a movie. Or we'd watch a few shows on Netflix in the morning with some homemade breakfast and then do a little house painting in the afternoon. We felt like we struck a great balance of accomplishment and relaxation. Maybe you can't pull off a true vacation, but you could probably manage some sort of hybrid!

Day-to-Day Life
Dates and vacations are great, but married couples need to prioritize spending time together and set time aside to make each other feel valued on a daily basis as well. It's true that we spend a lot of time together naturally these days. When either of us finishes work, even a later evening or a weekend shift, we head home to the house we share. We don't have to carve out time like we did when we were dating and our schedules didn't mesh well, but we still have to ensure togetherness is a priority.

When we got married, we wanted people to have the chance to share some of their "being married wisdom" with us at our wedding. We realized couples who had been married for forty-plus years would be there and were bound to have some great insights to pass along to us. At our reception, we set out an old, decorative suitcase for people to put their wedding cards into, but we also placed pens, paper, and a little card asking people to share their words of wisdom about marriage.

Marriage: Five Years Later

Note after note said almost the same thing:

Make sure you spend time together.

Keep going on dates!

Don't get so busy you forget to enjoy each other.

I was disappointed because I had been expecting some deeper insights gained from years of marriage! But we've come to realize that these comments *were* the hard-won wisdom. It came from years of trial and error, finding out what brings life to a relationship as well as what brings distance.

We actually saw the importance of this hard-won wisdom early in our marriage. While we were dating, Annaliese and I enjoyed grocery shopping together. We'd have a general idea of what we wanted to buy, taking our time finding the ingredients for whatever meal we were planning to make. But we wouldn't stop there; we'd notice the Double Stuf Oreos we obviously needed, and then the Hot Buffalo flavored pretzels, and then… You get it. We might also grab a new sauce from the international food aisle that we thought would add a nice flavor to a dish we'd eventually try. Those were some of the most fun (and expensive!) shopping trips we've ever experienced.

And Gentle

But now that we've been married for five years, the shine on grocery shopping is gone. We have a budget now, so spending money spontaneously on random snacks and sauces that we'll *maybe* use before they go bad doesn't seem like such a good idea anymore. And being more disciplined at the grocery store makes grocery shopping feel a whole lot more like a chore than like an outing!

Hilariously, when we were engaged, people would ask us what our favorite thing was to do together. I remember we said "Grocery shopping" at least one time. What we meant was that we enjoyed time together and we'd take it any way we could get it. But things change when routines and budgets get involved.

Another thing changed too. When we were dating and engaged, I thought Annaliese shared my love of NBA basketball. Sometimes she sat and watched full games with me, and she knew almost every player on a couple of teams. But, again, as time together became easier to come by, prioritizing something like watching a basketball game together became less and less important. I would go into the living room to watch a game, and she would go to her art room to work on a new crafting project. It completely makes sense that each of us would gravitate toward our own hobby, but it still threw me off at first. Even though I didn't have a desire to sit and watch her work on her crafting, for some reason I thought it would be nice if she'd come and watch a game with me.

But, again, these things change as life changes. It's not important to spend time together doing the exact same things you did when time together was hard to come by. What is important is that you find ways to keep spending quality time together.

Avoiding Damaging Behaviors

When we talk about being gentle in our marriage relationship, avoiding damaging behaviors is obvious. But it's worth spending some time on because many couples continually deal with this issue. Before any of us got married, we could go through life with the mentality that what we did in the realm of our thought life or our choices and actions shouldn't matter to other people all that much. That's because for the most part, when we were single, there *weren't* other people around to be hurt by what we did.

But marriage changes that. My life is now intertwined with Annaliese's in nearly every way. To put it in the words we see in Scripture, the two of us became one.

That means my justification *This won't hurt anybody else* is no longer true, if it ever was. So I need to be aware when potentially damaging thought patterns or behaviors show up in my life. The challenge is that I'm naturally so adept at justifying my questionable behavior in the moment. Aren't you? Think about how many times you've found yourself regretting an action after the fact and told yourself, *I'm not sure how that even happened. That's not what I wanted to do!*

I want to stop here, because I think honesty is the only way to move forward. What we really mean when we say *That's not what I wanted to do* is *Now that I've done that, I regret it.* Do you see how easy it is to use the first sentence to make ourselves feel better after we make a poor decision?

Let me give a personal example with a little backstory. Before Annaliese and I got married, we had the "porn conversation." We talked about how porn had been a part of both of our lives, but I flinched when she asked me how often I had looked at it. I didn't want to be honest in answering such a specific and concrete question, so my brain worked overtime to find a response that didn't sound so bad. I thought, *If I average the time over my entire life, the frequency won't sound so bad.* But I couldn't come up with anything that felt benign enough, so I

Marriage: Five Years Later

hemmed and hawed until we moved on to talking about how to manage any porn slipups in the future. We discussed how to keep each other informed and make sure we had accountability systems in place with the people around us.

I felt like I had dodged a bullet, and I got out of the conversation without ever lying, so that was a double bonus! The issue with that is the fact that our worst and most unhealthy habits thrive in secrecy. I had "successfully" avoided a difficult conversation and revealing more about myself than I wanted anybody—even Annaliese—to know, but I had set myself up to continue hiding and justifying.

Life went on like that for a few years. We got married, and I would still look at porn periodically, but I'd downplay it when I talked about it to Annaliese or my accountability partners.

All that changed when I started meditating regularly, a practice I detailed thoroughly in my first book, *Journeying with Pain*. I found that I couldn't spend time being quiet and letting God meet with me for long if I wasn't going to be obedient to him. For a week or two, I would sit and be quiet for thirty minutes, knowing I was going to spend that time feeling like I needed to have the porn conversation with Annaliese—the real one, the one where I stopped hiding. So naturally, I kept putting it off! That's what we do, isn't it? The worst imaginable thing is coming clean. But the weight of the secret just felt like it was building.

Then one evening in the middle of this period of time when I was resisting what I knew God wanted me to do, Annaliese and I were watching a movie. I started to feel like I needed to have the conversation right then. You know that feeling, right? My heart started to beat faster, and I felt tense and on edge. So I did what anybody would do: I just kept watching the movie! I even tried to convince myself I was feeling this way because the movie was so thrilling and exciting. It's crazy what we try to tell ourselves to avoid the truth.

Finally, I couldn't take it anymore, so I paused the movie and told Annaliese we needed to talk. I let her know I had convinced myself that I'd never "lied" to her about my history with porn, but that I hadn't been honest either. We had a thirty-ish-minute conversation that was uncomfortable and far more revealing about me than I wanted it to be. But it did something I never anticipated—it brought us closer! I'd been trying to keep a part of my life separate from her, which wasn't working because our lives were already intertwined. The truth that we had become one made more sense when I saw that my honesty and willingness to open up about something I preferred to keep hidden had brought us closer. It had connected us on a new level.

I tell this story to get back to the difference between *That's not what I wanted to do* and *Now that I've done that, I regret it*. For the longest time I told myself after looking at porn that it wasn't what I wanted to do. That comforted me and made me feel like there had been this brief, weird anomaly in my behavior, but now I was back to myself. But that wasn't true. The truth was that, in the moment, I did exactly what I wanted to do. But then came *Now that I've done that, I regret it*. That's how the descent into choices and habits I ultimately don't want for my life happens. I *don't* want this in the big picture, but I *do* want it in the moment.

Insight from Psalm 1

The challenging part is how easily we can become comfortable with things we never would've imagined ourselves doing. When I think of that, I think of Psalm 1, a sort of introduction to what the book of Psalms is all about. So many of the psalms are about the deep emotions of life, both the good and the bad and the distinction between where good choices lead and where bad choices lead. Psalm 1 aims to highlight that. The first chapter, in verses 1 and 2, starts this way:

> Blessed is the one who does not walk in step with the wicked or stand in the way that sinners take or sit in the company of mockers, but whose delight is in the law of the LORD, and who meditates on his law day and night.

The book of Psalms highlights the difference between living a righteous life and an unrighteous life, and the first two verses of the whole book tell us what will be repeated over and over. Something in these verses isn't immediately obvious, though—at least it wasn't to me. There's a progression of actions—from "walk[ing] in step with the wicked" to "stand[ing] in the way that sinners take" to "sit[ting] in the company of mockers."

The first time I came across this idea of a progression, I was confused. I thought the progression would be standing —> walking —> sitting. But the progression in the passage is walking —> standing —> sitting. I didn't get it until I started reading some commentaries on this passage. Walking in step with the wicked comes *before* standing because walking is the phase where we have plausible deniability. If we need to go from one place to another, we may end up either walking along with some people worth spending time with or around people we shouldn't spend much time around. And knowing human nature, we sometimes set it up so that we *accidentally* end up "walking" where we shouldn't. But we're just walking. It's most likely a complete coincidence—or at least we could convince other people of that.

Here's what it looks like for me to start "walking" down a path I know I shouldn't. I love watching basketball, and I'm a big NBA fan. I get the NBA League Pass every year, giving me access to almost every NBA game on my TV. I can also stream games if I'm not home. It's awesome! I stay up way later than a mid-thirties guy with an office job should. But it's my hobby, and I love it. I live in Michigan, so when the games on the West Coast start at 7:30 p.m. in their time zone, it's 10:30 p.m. for me. That means I'm up until 1:00 a.m. a decent number of nights throughout an average year. And since Annaliese is a normal, responsible adult, she's been asleep for a couple of hours by the time I head to bed.

"Walking" off the path for me usually happens in this late-night window. When the games are over, sometimes I'm not all that tired, especially if the game I was watching had an exciting ending. So I might start flipping through channels. Most of us know HBO, Cinemax,

And Gentle

and Showtime often have basically soft-core porn on in the early morning hours, but in that moment, I convince myself that it's okay to just flip through the channels to see if I can find something to watch. Never mind the fact that I could hit "Menu" and choose exactly what I might want to watch. I'll inevitably "accidentally" make it to one of those movie channels that could be in the middle of a show or movie with some nudity.

Do you see what I'm getting at? If anybody else was there to witness what happened, I would have some degree of plausible deniability. I could say I was just flipping through channels with no intention to see that. *Technically* I was just flipping through channels, but I know the true motivation behind that flipping, and I think that's what the psalmist is getting at. We're not doing anything too permanent at this phase, but we're comfortable flirting with the beginning of a bad decision.

Maybe this looks different for you. Maybe you're keeping a text conversation going with someone you're more attracted to than you'd be willing to admit. And even though you're just texting with him or her about some work stuff or about the soccer team both of your kids play on, you're keeping the conversation going longer than necessary because you enjoy the little jolt of electricity you get when the person messages you back. Deep down, you know why you're keeping that conversation going. That's what it looks like to be "walking in step with the wicked"—not that the conversation partner is the wicked one but that you (and I) are getting more comfortable with doing the wrong thing.

The next step is standing in the way sinners take. This is when you become more comfortable spending time doing something you would have initially been resistant to or would have felt more guilty about. This is taking the conversation into a more personal and intimate realm, into the world of an emotional affair. Or staying on the channel or pulling out the computer or your phone to make sure that if you're going to mess up, you're going to "get your money's worth."

The third step in walking off the path is sitting in the company of mockers. At this point, all pretense of a temporary fling is gone. You've pushed through that racing of the heart that indicates your conscience—or the Holy Spirit—is trying to tell you that you're heading down a path you shouldn't. You've moved from being uncomfortable and ashamed of what you're doing to deciding you don't care anymore. I doubt I'm alone in saying that I've experienced these moments when I was going to do what

I wanted to do without worrying about how it might hurt me, other people, or my relationship with God.

This transition is how we find ourselves in the middle of a behavior or a pattern of behavior that the three-years-ago version of us would be shocked to learn. It starts with small compromises, and if we get comfortable with minimally damaging behaviors and relationships, we put ourselves in a dangerous position of being more and more comfortable ramping up that behavior. Eventually we get to a place we can't believe we've traveled to, and we can't believe the damage we've done to our marriage.

Being Sensitive to Differences

Joining your life with another person is a big task. You're not just agreeing to be partners when it comes to paying the bills and sharing a living space; you're comingling your belongings, your design and decoration styles, your musical tastes, your spiritual habits, your chore schedules, and your grocery shopping and meal prep along with tons of other small, seemingly unimportant things. But when I say they're seemingly unimportant things, I'm talking about how we feel when it's still early in the relationship.

When Annaliese and I were dating, it was easy to write off her messy room because she had just one room to keep *all* her stuff in. And her habit of stacking clothes on the foot of the bed rather than hanging them up didn't bother me...when she was doing it at *her* house in *her* room. I was also way more tolerant of listening to what I call her "hipster music"—the indie and folk stuff she likes. I didn't really enjoy the music, but I didn't ask her to turn it off or turn it down around me.

In the same way, Annaliese never mentioned having a problem with my minimalist design tastes. Minimalist is my word for it; I think she'd use the word *barren*. Also, as I've already mentioned, we had fun going grocery shopping together when we were dating. We enjoyed whatever we were doing because we enjoyed being together. But these days grocery shopping isn't so fun. Over time we realized that we don't grocery shop the same way.

I like to make one big loop around the store and avoid doubling back to get something. I start out in the fruit and vegetable section, and then I head to the meats and go from there. Annaliese's grocery-shopping style is similar in some ways, but she's not as opposed to doubling back. We'll go down aisle 10 and then aisle 15, and then we'll double back to aisle 13 before going to aisle 18, and then we'll double back again to aisle 12. I don't know why, but this drives me crazy! Funnily enough, when it comes to driving anywhere, she's the one concerned with efficiency, and I'm more of a *it takes however long it takes* kind of guy.

I know these examples are simple and a little ridiculous, but they're probably reflective of conversations and frustrations that exist in your relationship too! What can get tricky is when we take it upon ourselves to "help" our spouse by "teaching" them to be more disciplined (or free spirited) in these small aspects of daily life. It can be tempting to double down on my home decoration aesthetic to make sure Annaliese sees the validity of my approach. Or to show her how much more efficient shopping could be if it's more of a well-planned trip. The problem is that we usually end up not validating ourselves but invalidating our spouse and their feelings and desires. Where is the gentleness in that?

Having that same attitude when it comes to bigger decisions does real damage. It's easier to just do what we want, and part of why this is so tempting is that it feels completely natural. And it is the most "natural" response, which is why actively practicing being gentle is so important for the health of our marriages.

CHAPTER THREE

Gentleness in Practice

Be completely humble and gentle; be patient, bearing with one another in love.
Ephesians 4:2

Probably the most significant piece of information Annaliese and I have come across in our relationship comes from the findings of psychologist Dr. John Gottman, who runs the Gottman Institute. Some of what I'm sharing about his work is outlined in an article from *The Atlantic*,[1] in which Gottman and his psychologist wife, Julie, are interviewed, and some of it is what I remember from other reading.

In the 1970s, divorce started trending in the United States and became more and more a potential outcome in many people's minds. In the following years, plenty of books and articles were written about the aftereffects of divorce based on studies done by social scientists. In those resources, you can learn about the economic impact of divorce on the two people involved in it, the emotional impact of divorce, and the impact divorce has on the kids whose parents get divorced. But in 1986, Gottman

---

[1] Emily Esfahani Smith, "Masters of Love," *The Atlantic*, June 12, 2014, https://www.theatlantic.com/health/archive/2014/06/happily-ever-after/372573/.

realized all these studies were reactive rather than proactive. They told us what happens *after* a divorce but not what happens *before* a divorce—what causes the divide that ends a marriage. He decided he wanted to know the answer to that question, so he met with couples before divorce was even a possibility for them.

He and his colleague, psychologist Robert Levenson, set up what they called "The Love Lab" at the University of Washington, where a team of researchers observed newly married couples interacting with each other as they were interviewed. They asked them the normal questions that we've all been asked as couples. Things like *How did you meet? How did you get engaged? What's a fun thing you did together recently? What's a point of conflict you've dealt with lately?* And because this was scientific research, they also hooked them up to equipment to measure their heart rates, blood flow, and sweat production. When they finished with the interviews, they organized the answers from the couples as well as their readings and measurements, but they didn't analyze the data. The plan was to follow up with these couples, all of whom seemed normal and happy, down the road.

Six years later, they found that some of the couples were thriving; they loved being around each other, and they were in a healthy place. These were the kind of relationships we're all working for. He called these couples the "masters." But not all the couples were doing well. Some of the relationships had ended in divorce. Some couples who were still married didn't have a healthy dynamic; they tolerated each other, but that was about the extent of it. He called these couples the "disasters."

Masters and disasters aren't the most creative designations in the world (Gottman is a scientist, after all!), but they are a helpful and easy way to make the distinction. Now that they knew which couples were healthy and which were unhealthy six years after the interviews, they looked at their initial results. A pattern emerged. Even though the couples had all seemed the same from an outside perspective six years earlier, their bodies had been telling a different story. The disasters had elevated blood flow, increased heart rates, and increased sweat production.

You probably remember a term for this from science or biology class a long time ago: fight-or-flight, the unconscious response you would have if you saw a bear or a leopard out in the wild. You'd freeze for a brief second and then feel your blood run cold and your hair stand on end. Then you'd have to decide: *What's my best chance for survival? Do I run, or do I stay and fight?* That's a completely normal response when you see a predator and you're in a vulnerable situation, but it's absolutely devastating to imagine feeling that way when you're around your husband or wife. Gottman and his team realized there must have been a larger pattern among the disaster couples. They must have been so used to being criticized, yelled at, or demeaned at a moment's notice that they were constantly on guard. They never knew when an attack might come. They went through life with their spouse in fight-or-flight mode because something could go down at any moment.

Can you imagine how hard that would be? Unfortunately, maybe you don't need to imagine it.

After they came to this conclusion, Gottman determined they still hadn't found the root of the issue. You can't just tell people "Don't be in fight-or-flight mode around each other" and send them on their way. He needed to do some digging to find out what brought couples to that point. In 1990, he set up a lab that resembled a bed and breakfast retreat and invited 130 couples to stay there for a few days, where they were observed as they went about their daily vacation routines (with their permission, of course!). For instance, the researchers watched as they had breakfast, planned their day, read the newspaper (remember, this was a while ago), and chatted about what they found there.

Gottman and his team realized all the couples did one thing whether their relationship was healthy or unhealthy, and they called it making a "bid for attention." This could be as simple as mentioning an article they were reading in the paper or talking about what they were interested in doing that day. *The Atlantic*'s article gives this example:

> Say that the husband is a bird enthusiast and notices a goldfinch fly across the yard. He might say to his wife, "Look at that beautiful bird outside!" He's not just commenting on the bird here: he's requesting a response from his wife—a sign of interest or support—hoping they'll connect, however momentarily, over the bird.[2]

As they watched these bids for attention, they saw another pattern emerging. When you share something you're interested in, the person you're sharing with gives you one of three responses (examples mine):

Positive:
"Thanks for sharing that!" "Wow, that's interesting, tell me more about that." "How do you know so much about this stuff?"

---

[2] Emily Esfahani Smith, "Masters of Love," *The Atlantic*, June 12, 2014, https://www.theatlantic.com/health/archive/2014/06/happily-ever-after/372573/.

Marriage: Five Years Later

Notice that you don't have to have a huge conversation about something for your response to be a positive one.

Neutral:

"That's nice." "Okay, great." "Glad you're happy."

Notice that the same words could be a positive or a blow-off response simply based on *how* they're said.

Negative:

"You know I don't care about that stuff." "Why would you waste your time telling me that?" Or complete silence.

These might seem tame to you. Or they might seem over the top. It will depend on what your life experience has been.

They categorized these responses into positive or negative categories, and they again saw a pattern emerge. The disasters gave their partners a positive response 33 percent of the time. The other two-thirds of their responses were neutral at best and belittling, negative, or combative at worst.

It doesn't take much imagination to realize what kind of impact this would have, does it? If I expected to feel like I was wasting Annaliese's time when I tried to share my life with her, I would be a lot more careful about what I brought up to her. Our shared world would get smaller and smaller as I became more and more aware of just how risky it was to let her know what interested me or brought me joy.

The masters had a much different ratio. They averaged an 87 percent positive response rate when their spouse made a bid for their attention. What a difference that would make! If I knew it would be rare to feel like Annaliese didn't care to hear about whatever was on my mind, I would be much more likely to share it even if it was a little strange. I'd know she provided a safe space, and she was open to sharing life with me.

What It Looks Like for Us

We all already know this, but inward focus destroys relationships, and outward focus makes them flourish. When I'm constantly thinking about how everything relates to me instead of about how it relates to us, I'm missing a huge piece of the puzzle. And that's what I'm doing if I'm ignoring or devaluing what matters to Annaliese or what she's interested in.

Here's one way that plays out for us. As I've mentioned before, Annaliese is a creative, artistic person. She's into fashion, and I'm not. When we first started dating, I felt weird that I wear jeans and a T-shirt or sweatshirt when we go out while she wears something that looks cool. Sometimes when I'm home and on the computer, browsing eBay looking for that next basketball card or checking up on NBA box scores or something else that's equally non-important, Annaliese will be looking at Pinterest or Etsy or something along those lines on her phone. Then she'll hold her phone out in my direction and say, "Hey, take a look at this _____" and show me a picture of a shirt. She won't call it a shirt. She'll call it a tunic top, or a cardigan, or a duster, or a mini high-low button up—I'm not making that up!—or some other term I'm not familiar with. There are probably over a hundred different names for what I would just call "shirts."

Then she'll ask me what I think of it, and that's a bid for my attention, a chance for me to practice responding in a positive way. I could be distracted or annoyed and say, "I'm looking at something else right now. You know I don't care about shirts." I could dismissively look over and say, "Yeah, looks fine." Or I could set my computer aside, take a look at what she's showing me, and say something about it. I don't have to *like* the shirt. I can be honest about that, and sometimes that's exactly what I do. I look at the shirt and tell her I'm not a fan of it. Other times I tell her I love the shirt she's found and that I think it would look great with some other piece of clothing or an accessory she has.

The point is that she's not really asking me if I care about a shirt; she's asking me if I care about *her*. And if I remember that when she's holding her phone out to me, it makes a huge difference!

But don't think our dynamic is that bids for attention come only from Annaliese. Because of me and my interests, she knows *way* more about the NBA than she ever wanted to in her life! I tell her when a guy signs a more lucrative contract than I expected him to. I tell her when somebody scores more points or gets more rebounds than I expected. I tell her Anthony Davis scored 40 points and got 15 rebounds last night, and she looks impressed before she asks, "What would be a normal amount?"

Annaliese even knows how to pronounce one of my favorite player's names. That doesn't sound all that impressive, but see if you can even guess how to pronounce this name: Giannis Antetokounmpo. Unless you've been watching a lot of ESPN, you're wrong. It's pronounced YAN-es AN-ten-ta-kum-bo. She can pronounce it better than a lot of the NBA announcers, and she makes fun of them for how badly they pronounce it! It's almost embarrassing to let you know how much it means to me that she can pronounce Giannis's name, but it genuinely means a lot to me. I know she doesn't care about Giannis; she's learned how to say his name because she cares about me.

Stuff like this happens every single day in a marriage. It happens with big, important things, and it happens with small, not-so-important things. And in those moments, we have the chance to give our husband or wife a positive response. Gottman had this to say about the bid for attention:

> There's a habit of mind that the masters have... which is this: they are scanning [their] social environment for things they can appreciate and say thank you for. They are building this culture of respect and appreciation very purposefully. Disasters are scanning the social environment for partners' mistakes.[3]

That line echoes a passage from Philippians 2:3–5. Paul writes,

> Do nothing out of selfish ambition or vain conceit. Rather, in humility value others above yourselves, not looking to your own interests but each of you to the interests of the others. In your relationships with one another, have the same mindset as Christ Jesus.

---

[3] Emily Esfahani Smith, "Masters of Love," *The Atlantic*, June 12, 2014, https://www.theatlantic.com/health/archive/2014/06/happily-ever-after/372573/.

Gentleness in Practice

I want to highlight the phrase "not looking to your own interests" because that's the one that jumps out in light of the research the Gottman Institute conducted. And, interestingly, the word translated *looking* is from the same root word as the word to describe a scout or a sentry that would keep watch from the city walls. The sentry's job was to keep an eye on whatever was happening around them, to be alert for both good and bad things coming on the horizon. When Paul writes about "looking out" for the interests of others, he's not talking about glancing around. He's talking about scanning your environment for the good of the people around you, just like Gottman talks about two thousand years later. This is not a new idea; this is what has kept relationships flourishing for centuries!

It's also interesting that Gottman says that *both* the masters and the disasters are scanning their environments. The question isn't if we will be scanning our environment in our relationship; the question is what we'll be looking for. If we're working to create a healthy dynamic, we're not constantly looking for our partner to fail so we can be right, so we can say we *knew* he would lose his phone or that she would leave the light on or that he would forget to feed the dog.

Just imagine the difference between that and knowing your partner is constantly on the lookout for things about you they appreciate! Obviously, living out that kind of gratitude and positivity takes some real effort, especially for those of us who are mostly practical, like me. It's been an adjustment, because I feel like it's kind of condescending to praise or thank Annaliese for something that didn't take a substantial amount of effort. I'm more than happy to praise her accomplishments and her ideas, but it's a lot harder for me to compliment her on little things that don't seem like they are "above and beyond."

But Gottman and Philippians 2 remind me that we're all scanning. We're all looking out for *something*. And if what we're on the lookout for are chances to critique, tweak, and outright criticize, we'll create an environment where our partners feel like being around us is a potentially dangerous situation. They're going to be living in fight-or-flight mode just waiting for the other shoe to drop. They don't know the next thing we might be annoyed by, but they know from past experience that they need to be ready for it.

It doesn't highlight the idea of scanning in the same way, but Eugene Peterson's paraphrase of this passage in Philippians 2 says "Don't be obsessed with getting your own advantage. Forget yourselves long enough to lend a helping hand" (MSG). If we practice that in our relationships, every one of our marriages will be changed for the better.

CHAPTER FOUR

Be Patient

*Be completely humble and gentle; be patient,
bearing with one another in love.*
Ephesians 4:2

Patience is a challenging piece of all relationships, and that's mostly because you don't need to be patient when everything is going your way. In fact, the encouragement to be patient has the built-in assumption that things aren't going your way. Working through our own selfishness is not the theme of marriage, but marriage does a great job of highlighting our tendency toward focusing on ourselves. We find ourselves frustrated by life circumstances as well as by the words or silence and actions or inactions of our partner. Some challenges are more insignificant, like addressing driving or grocery-shopping preferences, and some are more significant, like sticking to a budget or deciding whether to have kids or move out of state for a career change. Agreeing to share life with somebody else guarantees there will be inconveniences, frustrations, and conflict because we're not always going to be on the same page about how to manage every aspect of life.

One of my favorite examples of what a lack of patience looks like is from, of all places, Wikipedia, the online user-created encyclopedia. Because content is user-created, multiple users often have conflict over details in some of the articles. A page called "Wikipedia:Lamest edit wars" has some hilarious write-ups about the history of conflicts as multiple users/editors attempted to update the articles the way they felt was most appropriate. I could probably read about these edit wars for hours because it makes me laugh to see how dumb some of these disagreements are. It's hilarious to imagine the people sitting down to fight it out, one edit at a time. Here are a few of my favorites:

The synopsis of a debate about daylight saving time:

- "Or daylight savings time. Or Daylight Saving(s) Time. Or Daylight-Saving(s) Time. You've never heard 'saving' in the singular in your entire life? Send in the dualling (or is it duelling?) dictionaries."

Debate between the American spelling *aluminum* and the British spelling *aluminium*. As you read this, keep in mind that this book is around 19,000 words:

- "As a gauge of the scale of this territorial feud, the talk page specifically devoted to this debate is over 40,000 words of um/ium debate."

Debate over the entry for The Beatles:

- "An edit war over the order in which the four members of the group should be listed. Should they be listed in the 'traditional' order or in alphabetical order? And if you think that's ridiculous, edit wars over whether to identify the band as 'The Beatles' with a capital T or 'the Beatles' with a lower case t *have gone on longer than the group's existence*." (I added the emphasis there).

On Arachnophobia:

- "Is it appropriate to include a huge picture of a tarantula for illustrative purposes on a page discussing the fear of spiders?"[4]

I had a much longer list for you, but you get the point! So many of these entries had me laughing out loud. And as funny as it is to see the ridiculous things people are willing to argue over, it's important to see how easy it is to lose perspective on what really matters in the middle of an argument. I'm guessing that almost everybody reading this has had debates or arguments that dragged on

---

[4] "Wikipedia:Lamest edit wars," https://en.wikipedia.org/wiki/Wikipedia:Lamest_edit_wars

for years even if they were about things that could never be proved. I had a more-than-five-year debate with a college friend about a hypothetical situation we both knew had a 0 percent chance of ever being provable. It was as silly as some of these Wikipedia edit wars (or worse).

In those moments, practicing patience is probably the last thing any of us would feel like doing! And even though it's hard, I can tell you that for Annaliese and me, figuring out how to practice being patient with each other (remember, patience is only necessary when things aren't going the way we want them to go) has been huge for our relationship.

When Life Is Tiring

We came up with a way to remind ourselves to be patient with each other after spending a week together at a family camp where we both had many roles. I didn't grow up camping, either in tents or in pop-up campers, so even being in a cabin is more "roughing it" than what I prefer. When it's for a good cause, I can do it, but it still takes a toll on me. And while there, I was speaking twice a day and running from one event to the next with the kids and families. Annaliese's schedule was similar to mine, but instead of speaking, she was leading a small group. It was a good but shockingly tiring week for both of us.

When it came time to make the three-plus-hour drive home, we were completely drained. The drive itself went well, but we both realized we were run down and on edge. Even though we hadn't had a conflict up to that point, we could both sense one was coming. You know that feeling, right? When you aren't arguing…*yet*. Neither of us had said anything that rubbed the other the wrong way quite enough to cause conflict, but it was just a matter of time.

Instead of waiting and letting it all boil over, we had a conversation. We talked about how we were tired, run down, and more edgy than normal and would be quicker to take something the wrong way. What we came up with to remind ourselves to be patient is so simple that it's almost embarrassing to share, but it truly worked! Whenever we said something that might seem critical or negative or hurtful, we added "I mean well." I think it worked because it made me stop for just a moment and ask myself, *If she didn't mean that in a negative way, what could she have meant instead?* And Annaliese asked herself the same thing about me. This was a built-in reminder to be patient with each other.

We used that method *a lot* during the week immediately after camp because it took us more than a day or two to get back to our physical and emotional equilibrium. After we started feeling more normal, we didn't need to keep reminding each other that we meant well as often, but to this day, we sometimes add this request for patience from each other: "I mean well." It's a simple way we practice being patient with each other.

When Life Is Hard

Annaliese and I have also had a unique situation we've had to figure out how to deal with. If you've read my previous book, *Journeying with Pain*, this will be a review for you. But the backstory is that I've been dealing with a health issue since 2011, for roughly eight years at the time I'm writing this. I call it "a health issue" because I've never been able to get a diagnosis and I don't know what else to call it.

I feel dizzy and lightheaded all the time, a brain fog that never goes away. Sometimes it's worse than normal, but it's always there, every day. I feel like I got one hour of sleep the night before, every day. You know that feeling like everything is moving in slow motion around you and it takes a huge amount of effort to focus on what people are saying and doing? When it hits me hard, I even feel like I'm about to pass out. But although I've had tunnel vision many times, I've never lost consciousness.

Obviously, that list of symptoms has been tough to deal with. But on top of that, I've had tons of blood work and too many x-rays and MRIs, and I've seen many specialists, including an allergist, a neurologist, a cardiologist, a rheumatologist, a sleep specialist, and naturopaths trying to track down whatever bizarre thing is causing these symptoms.

As you can imagine, after a couple of years of dealing with this unknown condition but never having a meaningful update for people who asked me how I was feeling, I got pretty sick of talking about it and answering questions. So many well-meaning people have suggested what might be causing my issues, and I know they're trying to help, but I've tried so many things that I've arrived at the conclusion that this is something I'm just going to have to live with. And I know people don't mean it this way, but when they ask me about my health, it feels like they might as well be asking, "Hey, can we talk about the worst part of your life for a while?" That's how I interpret it, because I've had the same conversations countless times, and they never result in resolution or consolation. They just leave me feeling like the scab has been ripped off my wound, and I'm worse off than I was before the conversation. It can feel like I'm having the conversation for the sake of the other person—and that's hard when you feel like you're the one who should be comforted!

So I just started shutting people out. I refused to talk about my health in any meaningful way. If someone brought it up, I gave minimal responses but made it clear I didn't want to talk about it. I don't need to be reminded of it on a regular basis.

But I also shut Annaliese out. Of course, I didn't at first! When we started dating, I had already been dealing with this for a couple of years, but I gladly made an exception for her. We brainstormed what could be causing my condition and some potential doctors and specialists I could see. After a while, though, I began to feel the same way. After these conversations with Annaliese, I would feel more down and discouraged than I had before we started. I didn't have it in me to talk about it anymore, so I felt justified in stopping. I think I communicated that I was done, but it wasn't a discussion; I made the decision and made her figure out how to deal with it. She would still bring it up sometimes, but I shut down emotionally when she did. She would also talk about how hard this was for *us*. Whenever she mentioned that, I would get offended and ask what she meant about this affecting *us*. *I* was the one dealing with it!

Be Patient

It was a couple of years into our marriage before I fully realized I had been misunderstanding what marriage is. If two become one and we were supposed to be a team, I was messing up! I was acting like something in our lives could affect only me, but that didn't work for two people sharing life together. What affected me also affected Annaliese. And when I finally got that, it changed my perspective on our relationship and strengthened our marriage.

But it wasn't like flipping a switch. Change rarely is.

I let Annaliese know I had been messing up, which she of course already knew! I also told her I was committed to doing better, but it would have to be gradual; I couldn't go from 0 to 60 quickly, but I could have one conversation about my health each week—as long as it was only ten minutes long, at most. The ten-minute time limit would help me avoid feeling trapped into having one of these conversations last for a really long time and allow me to be more present in the moment as well.

So that's what we started doing. These conversations were long overdue because of my resistance to having them, but now she finally had the freedom to ask questions she'd been nervous to bring up because of how I would likely react. She got to ask about how I was feeling about having no answers, about how my health situation would affect us and the future, and about any potential next steps on my radar.

As tough as it was for me to have those conversations, after we did, I realized how important they were for us. I realized that I'd been holding Annaliese at arm's length after committing to sharing my life with her. And I realized how much damage it had done along the way and how much damage it was still doing. She'd felt like I didn't trust her to address my pain gently and that I didn't value her input. That wasn't what I meant to do; I was just trying to keep putting one foot in front of the other. But I had chosen a hurtful and damaging way to compartmentalize this part of my life, and I had cut her out. Whether or not I want this weird health thing to be a part of my life, it is. And because it affects my life, even though I wish it didn't, it affects hers too.

If you've been holding your spouse at arm's length when it comes to some hard aspect of your life—the state of your mental health, your hopes and dreams for the future, or some other area you think you're protecting yourself by not sharing—learn from my mistake and stop shutting your partner out! Trying to manage on your own is based on a misunderstanding of what marriage is all about, and it won't give you the solution you're looking for.

CHAPTER FIVE

Bearing with One Another in Love

Be completely humble and gentle; be patient, bearing with one another in love.
Ephesians 4:2

I'll start this chapter on a lighter note by sharing one of my favorite stories from early in our marriage—with Annaliese's permission. I wouldn't be writing this book if we didn't both believe in the value of sharing our learning experiences no matter how dumb and embarrassing the circumstances surrounding them. And these circumstances were *really* dumb and embarrassing: we had a conflict over a pizza.

If you know Jet's Pizza, you know they make what they call an eight-corner pizza. The best part is their crust, so they focus on it and make each of the eight pieces of pizza a corner piece. That means you get basically two pizzas, each shaped like a square. When we opened the box and saw our pizza, one slice was calling my name! You know the one. The pepperonis were dark and a little crispy around the edges, there was a generous amount of cheese, and it was one of the biggest slices in the box. I had my eye on it.

And then Annaliese grabbed it.

I'm not one to focus too long on a loss, however, so I found my "back up" piece. It was part of the other pizza, but as I was waiting for her to move aside so I could grab it, she reached out and grabbed that one too! She could tell I wasn't happy, but she didn't know why. So I explained I'd figured we were doing a "draft." She had the first pick, and she chose the obvious best piece. Fine. But that meant the next pick should have been mine. Yet she went for a second piece before I could take my first one. And even if we weren't drafting, she had claimed "her" pizza out of the two square pizzas by picking a slice from one of them.

Believe it or not, this conflict took us about forty-five minutes to work through. And if you're thinking it's ridiculous how big of a deal we made about a pizza, you're right! That's the whole point. What we end up having the biggest moments of conflict over are often the things that matter the least in the big picture. I bet that's true for most of the people reading these words right now. In those moments, however, we have the chance to practice bearing with one another in love.

We've chosen to deal with this conflict over pizza by making it a long-running joke. I do most of the cooking, so when I finish making a meal, I divide the food onto two plates and then let Annaliese know dinner is ready and it's her chance to "draft" the plate or bowl she'd like. We probably joke about "drafting" a meal three or four times a week. It's a dumb joke that has probably dragged on for too long, but it's our way of taking the teeth out of the Jet's Pizza conflict and making sure we don't take little things too seriously.

I'm guessing you have your own version of the drafting food conflict. And I'm not saying that making light of it is the way to go for everybody, but it's worked for us. It's allowed us to take what shouldn't have been a conflict in the first place and reminded us to approach this situation in a lighthearted way. I encourage you to find some way to take the teeth out of your own small, repeated, don't-really-matter conflicts too! That's what it looks like to bear with one another when it comes to the small stuff.

When Your Way Feels "Normal"

When it comes to things that are more important or that affect more of our lives, though, it's a whole lot harder to practice Paul's teaching. During these first five years we've realized we've both been influenced by our family of origin more than we initially thought. The environments we both grew up in seem "normal" to us. I put the word *normal* in quotes because no single definition of what normal or ideal looks like for a family unit exists. Behaviors both healthy and unhealthy absolutely play out in every family and in every marriage, but lots of things can be done in lots of different ways and still be perfectly healthy. You've probably run into some of this already.

For instance, I was taught the value of keeping the bathroom exhaust fan running to keep mold and mildew from forming. I probably took that to heart a little too much, because if it were up to me, I'd keep ours running all day after I shower in the morning. But Annaliese grew up in a home where "normal" behavior was to run the fan for a short time and then turn it off. Hearing it running all day just doesn't sit right with her. You see how what we did in our family of origin feels like the *right* way, don't you? When it's about bathroom fans or similar preferences, it's not too hard to figure out a compromise. But when those differences affect us on a deeper level, it's a whole different deal!

I noticed what I started to call the Dykstra Way—named for Annaliese's family of origin—early in our relationship. That's what I started to call the things that were "normal" for Annaliese because she grew up in the Dykstra family. And what was normal for her family stood out to me because it differed so blatantly from the Seaborn Way—named for my family of origin.

For instance, the Seaborn family deals with conflict through immediate confrontation and anger—when appropriate (and sometimes when it's not!). You know the saying that when you're holding a hammer, everything looks like a nail? That's the Seaborn family when it comes to confrontation. Did someone say or do something you don't like? Confront! Did someone just share an opinion you don't agree with? Confront! Did someone ask for an article of clothing for Christmas that isn't your style? Confront! That last one is only kind of a joke! You don't spend time with the Seaborn side of the family and leave wondering if you did something to offend somebody. If you did, you'll know.

That's the world I grew up in. The Seaborn Way is what feels normal to me. When Annaliese and I have moments of conflict, I don't shy away from confrontation. When it comes to conflict, I'm comfortable letting her know what I'm upset about. I can talk about what was said, how it made me feel, how it would've made me feel if it had been slightly different, and why it made me feel the way it made me feel. And there's nothing wrong with any of that.

But Annaliese grew up with the Dykstra Way, which in many ways is the opposite of the Seaborn Way. The first time I met her family, we weren't officially dating yet, and I immediately knew something was different from what I was used to. Her parents and her siblings hugged me and greeted me warmly; they were excited to meet me and get to know me. During that whole evening, I found myself thinking, *Why are they being so warm and over-the-top nice? They don't even know anything about me!* To be honest, it was a little disorienting.

As I learned more about the Dykstra family, though, it made more and more sense to me. The Dykstra Way is geared toward generosity and warmth. They want people to feel heard and understood in every conversation. They want to make sure people feel valued and like everybody is on the same page.

Do you see how our relationship felt like a clash of worlds in some ways? If we're not careful, during a conflict we can revert to our "normal" and feel completely alienated from each other. I can walk away feeling like Annaliese is trying so hard to find common ground that she's dancing around what needs to be said. I can think, *I just need her to be direct and truthful. Why is she lying?* And she can think, *I just need him to be more gentle and less blunt and straightforward. Why is he being a jerk?* You get how this can easily happen, right? And even though neither of us are doing anything *wrong*, if we continue to allow our families of origin to have undue influence over what we consider "normal," we're setting ourselves up for a 100 percent chance of conflict escalation.

When I write about the Seaborn Way and the Dykstra Way, I'm sure you're thinking about what your family's "Way" looks like. And I'm also sure some people reading this were handed some behaviors much more destructive and difficult to overcome. Remember that what you grew up in the middle of was normal for you. In other words, what you saw your parent(s), grandparent(s), foster parent(s) doing in their relationships and in their approach to the world seems like the right way until you come across information that challenges that. The Seaborn Way of dealing with conflict seems completely normal and right to me, but to Annaliese and many people reading this, it flies in the face of what they've been taught about interacting with people.

I've had to figure out how to grow through this as Annaliese and I have grown together. I had to learn how to take the good parts of what I'd been handed, and I have to continue to figure out how to leave the bad parts of what I've been handed behind.

You might be reading this and thinking, *Man, it would be so much easier to relearn conflict than to relearn some of the more major components of relationships.* Because if you grew up in a home with verbal, emotional, or physical abuse or with strict gender roles and expectations or ideas about where the authority comes from in a family, you probably went into your marriage with some expectations for what was "normal" in relationships that your spouse didn't share.

If you're dealing with some of those heavier issues, I highly recommend that you seek a counselor. An outside perspective from someone who is completely objective is incredibly valuable. Even without having been handed a warped sense of what's "normal," Annaliese and I both see counselors individually, and we see one as a couple as well. These sessions have been so helpful for both of us to learn more about ourselves, to see our own unhealthy patterns, and to evaluate how to move forward in a healthy way. If you're wrestling with the version of normal you've been handed, a counselor can be hugely helpful in untangling the good from the bad.

Think about it this way: if you don't deal with what's weighing you down from the past, you'll carry it into the future for far longer than you need to.

Hiding vs. Experiencing Freedom

This lines up with the way I understand Jesus's teachings, and a specific moment in his life from John 8 illustrates this idea perfectly.

As Jesus preached and taught about the kingdom of God, he upset a lot of the religious leaders. They thought he was a false teacher who was blasphemous for calling God his father and saying that he and his father were one. In several passages in the Gospels, the Pharisees and Sadducees try to catch Jesus saying something they can use against him. John 8 is one of those passages. As Jesus is teaching publicly, they bring a woman who had been caught in adultery. Think about that for a moment. If the woman was "caught," a second person was involved. But they didn't bring that person along. They just brought her, which is one of the signs that they were using her as a prop to make their point. Then they publicly challenged Jesus with a question: "Teacher, this woman was caught in the act of adultery. In the Law Moses commanded us to stone such women. Now what do you say?" (John 8:4–5).

Verse 6 spells it out in case we missed what was going on: "They were using this question as a trap, in order to have a basis for accusing him." This was especially disingenuous, because the death penalty for adultery had fallen out of favor with the Jewish people and was rarely practiced.

They used that as their leverage, and they put him into a position where he had to make a definitive statement that would cause issues either way. If he said she should be stoned, he would certainly lose the reputation he had earned from being a "friend of sinners" and from teaching so often about grace and love. But if he said she should not be stoned, he would be directly contradicting what was written in the Scriptures. If he did that, they would have him caught, because he couldn't really be a teacher of the Scriptures if he chose to ignore what they said. He was facing a lose-lose situation. He could either extend grace and be seen as ignoring God's Word or affirm the law and lose so much about his teaching that had made him captivating and arresting as a leader.

Faced with this dilemma, he chose an interesting first step. He knelt and wrote in the dirt with his finger, but they kept pressing him until he finally answered them. Instead of making a definitive statement, he said that whoever in the crowd had never sinned should be the one to throw the first stone. And then he knelt again and continued writing in the dirt. John didn't record what he was writing, but scholars have some theories. Some think he was writing out the sins this woman's accusers had committed. Some think he was writing the accusers' names because Jeremiah 17:13 says "Those who turn away from you will be written in the dust because they have forsaken the LORD." Others think he was writing in the dirt just to show them that he didn't have interest in what they were saying.

Maybe it was a combination of what he was writing and what he had said, but the accusers began to leave one by one. When no one was left, Jesus got up and asked the woman,

"'Where are they? Has no one condemned you?'

'No one, sir,' she said.

'Then neither do I condemn you,' Jesus declared. 'Go now and leave your life of sin'" (John 8:10–11).

In this response to someone who wasn't living life in line with God's plans, Jesus made it clear that God's rules and guidelines don't exist because he loves to punish us, to rub our faces in our mistakes. That's the attitude we see from the religious leaders in this passage. They view their faith as a bunch of rules for people to obey so they can avoid being punished. But when we see God's rules and standards as his attempt to command and control us, we cover up our shortcomings and go out of our way to protect our public-facing image. We want to carefully guard the truth about ourselves, because if people knew what we were really like or what we really thought, we'd be exposed and punished.

Instead of that approach, Jesus meets this woman with grace and compassion. His goal is that she leaves her destructive behaviors behind. He doesn't condemn *her*, but he also doesn't pretend everything is fine about the way she's been living. He tells her to leave her life of sin as she goes. His motivation is not to punish and harm her but to help her experience freedom.

I believe that, in the same way, God wants to offer us freedom moving forward. But the first step in this process is the worst part, *the exposure of a fault*. If we have the religious leaders' view on sin and mistakes, we'll make every effort to avoid the exposure of any shortcomings or flaws because we view that exposure as what happens right before the swift judgment and punishment come. But Jesus's response was the opposite. The exposure of the fault was the key step in the process that allowed correction and healing to take place. It requires a massive amount of trust—in both God and in our partner—to allow something of ourselves to be exposed.

This is so hard because it's the opposite of what most of us have been practicing for as long as we can remember. Think about how hard we work to keep our flaws from being exposed. We try on article after article of clothing to find the most flattering look, we delete selfie after selfie so we're left with a couple that were taken from just the right angle (and then we add a filter to those pictures!), and we clean and organize our homes before having company. Certainly, none of these things are bad or wrong, but think about what they all have in common. We're trying to highlight the positive things about us while we minimize or hide the negative things. When it comes to spirituality and vulnerability, the opposite is what we need to start doing. We need to let our spouse see our flaws and shortcomings. We need to admit them to God. And we don't do that so we can receive the punishment we deserve; we do it so we can experience correction and healing and freedom.

If you're going to open up and genuinely experience intimacy, whether in your marriage or in your relationship with God, you have to stop hiding. Allowing the truth about yourself to be fully exposed is scary, but intimacy is about being fully known and fully loved, and there's no shortcut to that destination. You have to do the hard work of opening up and letting parts of yourself (even parts that aren't flattering) be known by your spouse.

The reasoning here is twofold. First, as I've been saying and as Jesus's interaction with this woman illustrates, the exposing has to happen before the correction and healing can take place. Second, if you continue to hide, you put limits on the shared life you have with your partner. If you're hiding, you end up in positions where you may have to lie to keep the concealment going, or you can't leave your phone lying on the counter, or you have to avoid genuine conversations after a church service where something said touched a nerve. Hiding is *tiring*!

As I mentioned in the section about porn, I know this from firsthand experience. Anytime Annaliese and I were watching a movie or TV show that had a plot that mentioned porn in any way, I was on pins and needles hoping Annaliese wouldn't say anything about it! Anytime the sermon at church was about lust, I drove home trying to come up with *anything else* to talk about. Even though hiding is tiring and uncomfortable and awful, we opt for it way too often. It's our natural response to keep our faults and flaws and weaknesses from being exposed. But God invites us into the opposite of that! He invites us to a better way.

When we stop hiding and start being honest, that's just one more way we figure out what it means to "bear with one another in love." Through the good and the bad, the easy and the hard, the fun and the work, we're in this together!

CHAPTER SIX

Living It Out

*Be completely humble and gentle; be patient,
bearing with one another in love.*
Ephesians 4:2

It's my hope and prayer that you've seen yourself and your own marriage reflected in these pages—in both the good and the bad. And I believe that as we practice being completely humble and gentle, being patient, and bearing with one another in love, we'll grow closer to our partners and our marriages will flourish.

One of the unexpected benefits of growing in your marriage is that many of these same lessons will be immediately applicable to your other relationships as well. That seems obvious, but it caught both Annaliese and me off guard. We've both realized that in practicing these things with each other, our other relationships are affected as well. Once I realize that some of the conflict between Annaliese and me is a result, in part or in full, of a misunderstanding or miscommunication, I'm forced to realize that might be what's happening in some of my other relationships too.

I've found that as I've grown in my willingness and ability to be patient in my marriage, I make much more of an effort in all my relationships to be patient, to see things from other people's perspectives, and to give grace in moments of frustration, conflict, and misunderstanding. As I've grown in my willingness and ability to be gentle in my marriage, I find myself taking an extra moment before responding harshly to other people as well. As I mentioned in the very beginning of this book, Ephesians 4:2 isn't even *about* marriage; its lessons are about relationships. And it only makes sense that those lessons will make the most impact in our closest and most intimate relationships. As we practice living this verse out in our marriages, we find that what we're intentionally practicing and being mindful of will show up in unexpected places throughout our day.

In closing, I want to give one final plug for counseling. As I've mentioned before, applying these lessons is much harder than writing about them or reading about them. And it will be perfectly normal to run into something in your marriage that the two of you just can't figure out how to navigate in a healthy way. At times your needs will seem to directly contradict your partner's needs. At moments neither of you will be able to find the right words to achieve understanding. Sometimes what seems "normal" because of your family of origin will run right up against what your partner views as "normal." I could go on, but you get the point. You've probably *lived* the point. We sure have!

If you run into something like that, don't think you're the only couple who has. As I said in the Introduction, Annaliese and I have been surprised at how common many of these challenges are as we've talked with other couples in their first several years of marriage. The process of two different people trying to figure out how to integrate their lives isn't simple or straightforward! The key is to remember that it's never you *against* your spouse when it comes to conflicting or competing needs or wants; it's you and your spouse *together* working to figure out how to overcome the barriers that are just part of life.

Doing that means you'll have some tough conversations along the way, because figuring out how to speak each other's language doesn't always come naturally. And I can't tell you the road will be smooth all along the way. But I can tell you it's worth it! Let's go and "be completely humble and gentle; be patient, bearing with one another in love."